Fire Stick:

Easy to Advanced Tips and Tricks to Get the MOST Out of Your Device, an In-Depth PICTURE Guide for ALL! (Streaming Devices, Amazon Fire TV Stick User Guide, how to Use a Fire Stick

Table of Contents

Introduction

Chapter 1: Understanding What the Amazon Fire Stick Is

Chapter 2: What's in Your Fire Stick Box?

Chapter 3: Setting Up Your Fire Stick Once It's Plugged In

Chapter 4: Streaming Shows on Your Device

Chapter 5: Alexa and the Amazon Fire Stick

Chapter 6: Tips on How to Get the Most from Your Fire Stick Device

Chapter 7: The Controversial Kodi Application and How to Use It

Conclusion

interim quality. Trademarks that are mentioned are done without written consent and can in no way be considered an endorsement from the trademark holder.

Introduction

Congratulations on downloading *Fire Stick: Easy to Advanced Tips and Tricks to Get the MOST Out of Your Device, an In-Depth PICTURE Guide for ALL! (Streaming Devices, Amazon Fire Stick User Guide, how to Use Fire Stick)* and thank you for doing so. This book will guide you through everything that you need to know about purchasing and using an Amazon Fire Stick. After you read this book, you will have absolutely no trouble navigating the ins and outs of all of the aspects that the Fire Stick can offer you. What's more, you won't be forced to read a boring manual guide in order to learn everything that is essential to operating your device like a pro. This book will tell you everything that you need to know while also keeping things interesting.

The following chapters will discuss what exactly the Fire Stick is and does, the steps that you need to take in order to set up your device, how Amazon has incorporated Alexa into the Fire Stick capabilities, and so much more. If you are someone who is somewhat illiterate when it comes to technology, then you have certainly landed yourself in the right place by downloading this book.

There are plenty of books on this subject on the market, thanks again for choosing this one! Every effort was made to ensure it is full of as much useful information as possible, please enjoy!

Chapter 1: Understanding What the Amazon Fire Stick Is

Before we dive into all of the great things that the Amazon Fire Stick can do, you must first understand what exactly the Amazon Fire Stick is. This chapter will include basic information on the qualities of this device, including its price, the two different models that are available for purchase, and how these models differ from one another. With a basic understanding of the basics of the Fire Stick, you'll know exactly how much you'll be spending when you invest in either option of the provide that Amazon makes.

What is the Amazon Fire Stick?

As the picture above depicts, the Amazon Fire Stick can literally fit into the palm of your hand. This device, while small, can offer your television a wide variety of options. At its core, the purpose of the Fire Stick is to enable an older television to become a smart television. A smart television is one that is connected to the internet. When you own a television that's connected to the internet, you're able to access applications such as Netflix, Amazon Prime, and Hulu. Amazon released the Fire Stick in 2014 so that they could compete with services that Google and Roku were both offering their customers. These types of devices are collectively known as streaming TV sticks, because of their ability to stream television shows and movies directly into your home via an internet connection.

The Fire Stick's Voice Remote Option

In addition to providing a streaming service to their customers, Amazon also came out with a voice remote option for their Fire Stick in 2016. While we will discuss this option is much more depth in a subsequent chapter, this additional service allows you to speak to your remote control and tell it what to do. This means that instead of having to flip through the various channels with your remote control, you can simply speak into the remote and say, "Turn on Game of Thrones" (if you have an HBO subscription), or tell it to play a movie that you'd like to watch. Again, we will get into how exactly you can acquire this type of remote in a later chapter, but it's primarily important to know that you are able to invest in this type of feature if it's something in which you're interested.

The Amazon Fire TV

In addition to the small USB-like device that is the Amazon Fire Stick, Amazon also came out with a small TV box that is available for purchase. While more expensive than the Amazon Fire Stick, the Amazon Fire TV is designed to be more of a traditional cable box than is the Fire Stick.

Pictured above, if you have ever seen an Apple TV then you can probably tell that Amazon likely produced this device in response to the development of Apple TV. While the Fire Stick and the Amazon TV are similar in the sense that they can provide your television with the same functions, the qualities that the Fire TV can provide that the Fire Stick cannot include more memory storage and faster internet access. Additionally, the Fire TV enables its users to plug other cords and cables into the Fire box, whereas the Fire Stick does not provide this capability. While it is beyond the scope of this book to discuss the Fire TV in great detail, it's useful from a consumer perspective to know that you can purchase an Amazon TV that is essentially an enhanced version of the Fire Stick. If you're looking for something that is practically-priced and will largely meet your entertainment needs, the Fire Stick is sure to accomodate you nicely.

What Does the Fire Stick and the Fire TV Cost?

Now that you largely know a few of the advatanges to purchasing both the Amazon Fire Stick and Fire TV, let's talk about cost. Often, cost is one of the most important factors in determining whether or not you're going to purchase a product, and this makes sense. The chart below compares the price of the Fire Stick with the price of the Fire TV, along with some other important specifications that you can consider:

	Fire Stick	Fire TV
Cost	$39.99	129.99
Memory Capabilities	1 gigabyte	2 gigabytes

As you can see from the table above, the Fire TV costs significantly more money than does the Fire Stick; however, you're getting more memory and additional application capabilities when you purchase the Fire TV. If cost is your primary motivator, then certainly the Fire Stick is going to look more attractive to you then will the Fire TV; however, if you're a gamer or someone who is going to be saving a lot of shows on your device, then the Fire TV may be the better option. Regardless of the device that you end up choosing, it's obvious that money is a big deciding factor. If you're still not sold on the relevance of the Amazon Fire products, it might be a good idea to consider the fact that you're proably paying close to the cost of the Fire TV right now to your current cable provider. When you consider all of the television shows that you don't even end up watching that are available to you through services such as Comcast or Verizon, you may start to realize that the idea of having a television that is connected to the internet rather than connected to a cable box is the more useful option.

Hopefully, this chapter has provided you with a basic understanding of how both the Fire Stick and the Fire TV operate, and may even get your wheels turning in considering why these types of products might be ones that can help you to save money. The simple fact of the matter is that more and more people are deciding to switch to using services like the Fire Stick and Fire TV because the cost of cable is too high. Additionally, it can definately be argued that the majority of shows that are worth watching can only be found through internet-subscription services such as Netflix and Amazon Prime. These Amazon products are evidence to the fact that the future of television is changing. The internet has become more important than cable in terms of entertainment value. If you resist the change that is occuring in this sector, you will likely fall behind not just from a technological perspective, but also a cultural perspective, too.

Chapter 2: What's in Your Fire Stick Box?

While the first chapter should have provided you with some information on how the Fire Stick and Fire TV work, this chapter is going to focus on explaining everything that is contained within the Fire Stick product box. While Amazon and other types of companies who produced these types of products will often state their products are easier to install than ever before, the fact of the matter is that if you're someone who is relatively inexperienced with technology or do not know someone who can help you set up your devices, then you may not know exactly how to navigate very well. After reading this chapter, you will know exactly what it is that you're going to find inside of the Fire Stick product box, as well as what the buttons on your remote control do. The information in this chapter is quite extensive, so it will only explain the type of hardware that you're going to receive in the Fire Stick box. Chapter three will provide you with what you need to know once you've turned your television on and the Fire Stick is up and running on your screen. Obviously, this chapter has been written under the assumption that you have already gone out and purchased your Amazon Fire Stick. If you have not yet done this, it may be helpful to purchase the device prior to reading this chapter.

Installing Your Amazon Fire Stick

When you receive your Fire Stick, it's going to come in a relatively small, square-shaped box, and this box is depicted in the picture below.

This box is going to have a small sticker on it, that you're going to have to remove before you will be able to get to the actual product itself. Once you take this sticker off of the box, you should be able to slide the Fire Stick box away from the box that is holding it. This will reveal another box that can be opened by finding the flap at the bottom of the box when the direction of the box is facing you and you can read "Fire TV Stick" on the front of it.

Let's talk about the remote first. The remote is going to be relatively small and if you have ever seen an Apple TV remote, you will be able to realize that the Amazon Fire Stick remote looks extremely similar to it. The only exception between the two is that the Amazon Fire Stick remote appears to be a bit bulkier than the Apple TV remote, which will most likely help you to lose it less than you would an Apple TV remote. Your Fire Stick remote is going to require two AAA batteries, and the good news for you is that these batteries are included in the box with the rest of your Amazon streaming equipment.

The next piece of equipment that you're going to be dealing with after you handle the remote is the USB Fire Stick itself. This is also going to be wrapped in plastic, so be sure to remove this plastic prior to doing anything else with the device. The metal piece of the USB drive that Amazon has provided you will be where you plug in the Fire Stick to your television's HDMI port. If you're familiar at all with HDMI ports, this is the same place where an HDMI cable basically goes when you're looking to hook up your computer to your television for whatever reason. You may also notice that on one of the long sides of the Fire

Stick there is another port above the word "power". This is where your power supply will go so that the device will turn on. A photo of this port is shown below.

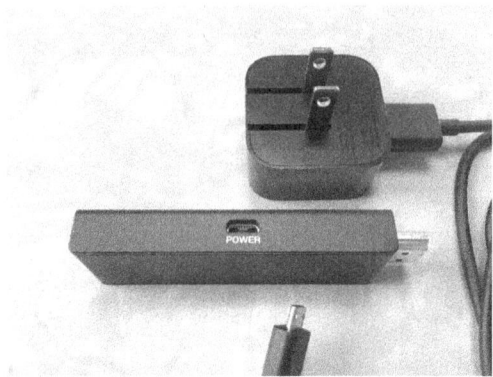

Once the Fire Stick and the remote control have been removed from the box, you are going to see an orange container that was previously holding these two pieces of equipment. Remove this packaging, and underneath you will see an instruction manual. Since you are reading this book, you will most likely not need this manual, but it's advised that you hold onto your manual at least until you're finished installing the Fire Stick. If you ever do need to use it, the instruction manual can serve as a user guide, a troubleshooting guide, and quick startup guide. Remove the manual from the box, and underneath of this you will find the two AAA Amazon batteries that can be used for your remote control, along with a power adaptor that connects to an additional USB cable so that your device will power on. It's important to note that this item is only the *adaptor* for the cable, not the cable itself. You will have to connect the adaptor to the cable on your own; however, Amazon does provide this USB adaptor cable for you, and it can be found next to the black adaptor in the box. Lastly, underneath of the power adaptor cable you will find an HDMI extension cable. Below you will see a photo of what this extension cable is going to look like, to eliminate any possible confusion.

You Have Your Equipment...Now What?

Now that you have guided pictures and additional information on what kind of equipment you will receive upon purchasing the Amazon Fire Stick, the next step in this process is to figure out how to put all of these pieces together. The first step that you want to do after you all removed all of your equipment from the package is to connect your USB power adaptor cable to the power adaptor. Once you've done this, you're then going to want to connect this cord to the Amazon USB Fire Stick, and then plug all of this into the outlet that is nearest your television. Before you plug your device into the power outlet, it should look identical to the picture that's below.

Once the power adaptor for the cord that you've put together is plugged into a source of power, the next step is to plug the USB Fire Stick into the HDMI port on your television. If you find that your cord isn't long enough to reach the HDMI port from the source of power, this is where that HDMI extension cable might come in handy.

Plugging in the Extension HDMI Cable

These instructions are not going to be for everyone, but if you do find yourself in a situation where the power cable is not long enough to reach the Fire Stick HDMI port to the HDMI television port, then you will need to use the HDMI extension cable that was provided for you in the Fire Stick box. From here, you don't have to remove anything from the current cable that you have already assembled. Instead, simply attach the female end of the HDMI cable to the male end of the Fire stick. Doing this should provide your cable with enough length to easily reach the power source to the television itself.

Your Fire Stick Remote Control Options

Before we dive deeper into how you can finish setting up your Fire Stick once it's been plugged into your television, it's important to understand how the remote control that you received with your product operates because this is the tool that you will use to complete the remainder of the installation on your television set.

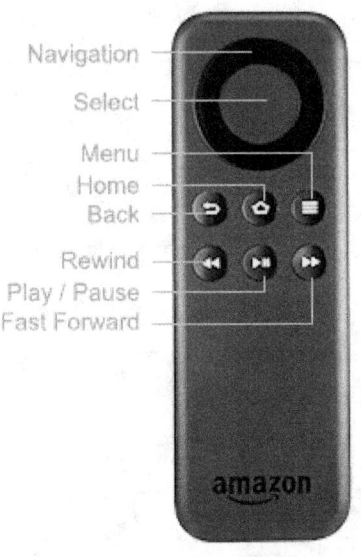

Navigation ─
Select ─
Menu ─
Home ─
Back ─
Rewind ─
Play / Pause ─
Fast Forward ─

As the photo above depicts, here are the basic options that you have when you're navigating the Fire Stick with your remote control. Obviously, this is not going to be rocket science if you've used a remote control for a regular television in the past, but it's still important to go over these features so that there is no confusion. For the setup, you're primarily going to be using the "Navigation" button and the "Select" button. What's most important to understand about the navigation button is that it is the *entire* darkened black circle, not just the top area of it as it is seen in the photo. This circle corresponds to the directions that you can move around on the television screen once your Fire Stick is up and running. For example, if you're at the home screen but are looking to fix a problem that is occurring with your internet connection and the settings option is located on the right side of the screen, you would want to press on the right outer edge of the navigation button, because doing this will move your mouse in literally the right direction. On the other hand, if you wanted to move away from the right side of the screen, all you would have to do is click on the left outer edge of the navigation circle. Whenever you get to where you want to go using the navigation button, the "Select" button will allow you to click on the option that you desire. The select button is the large black circle that is surrounded by the navigation circle.

While these are the buttons that are going to help you to set up your device, the "Back", "Home", and "Menu" buttons are all additional navigation buttons that are a bit more specific in nature. Obviously, the back button is pretty self-explanatory. The Home button will take you back to the Fire Stick home screen, which can be seen below.

The home screen will allow you to easily access any videos that you have saved, and will also help you to navigate to the type of entertainment you're seeking such as photos, games, movies, or television shows. Of course, you're most likely going to be using the home screen when you first turn on your device, but this button is also useful for when you're in a situation where you become bored with the show or movie that you're watching or quickly want to switch to a different form of entertainment. It's important to understand that the menu button is similar to the home button in the sense that this button will take you back to the different menu options that you see above in the photo. Both of these buttons make it easier to search for exactly what it is that you're to do on the Fire Stick with as much convenience as possible.

The last three buttons on the remote control should not require much of an explanation. If you've ever used a remote control for a DVD or even a DVR player, then you should already know that the rewind button will guide you back to the previous frame of a movie or a show that you'd like to rewatch, the play button should be pressed whenever you begin a show or a movie and this same button can be used in a situation where you want to keep the show on but want to take a break to use the bathroom or perform any other type of activity. The fast forward button can be considered to be the complete opposite of the rewind button in the sense that it will take you ahead in the show. This button is specifically useful when you've already watched part of a show or a movie and are looking to resume same place where you left off.

Chapter 3: Setting Up Your Fire Stick Once It's Plugged In

Now that you know about how all of the buttons on the remote control work, we can continue our conversation about how to set up your Fire Stick device once there is power to it and you can see it on your screen. This chapter is going to talk about all of the initial steps that you need to take before you can enjoy everything that the Fire Stick can offer you once it's properly been installed. By the end of this chapter, you will have all of the information that you need regarding all aspects of the Fire Stick set up process.

A Quick Note on Your Input Settings

After you've plugged your Fire Stick power adaptor into an outlet and have then connected the Fire Stick to the HDMI port on your television, you are going to want to make sure that your television is turned on; however, once your television is on, this still may not guarantee that you will be able to see the Fire Stick setup menu on your television set. It's important that you switch your television set to the HDMI input channel before you begin trying to setup your device on your television. Your television's remote will likely have a button on it that says "input". It's hard to say exactly where this button will be located on your remote because it is usually in a different spot depending on the television set that you have. Once you hit input, you will likely see a list of different options, and you should select the option that relates to an HDMI cable. If your television set has not preselected this option, then you are not going to see anything related to the Fire Stick show up on your screen, which is why having this knowledge prior to doing anything else related to your Amazon device is important.

The Fire Stick Screen Setup Process

Once you have navigated your television towards the correct input channel, you should be able to see the Fire TV Stick registration screen on your television. It will probably look like something along the lines of the picture below.

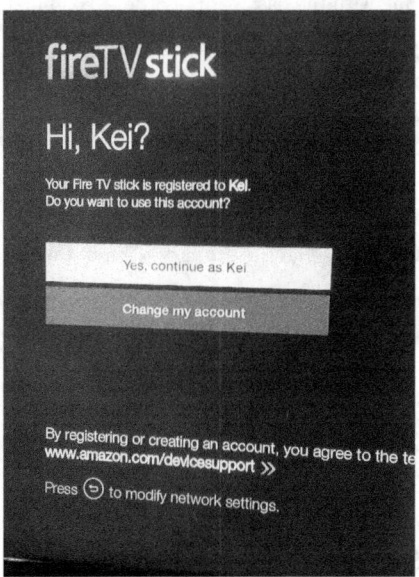

If you've purchased your Fire Stick directly through Amazon rather than a third party, then you will likely see your name next to the "Hi" instead of "Kei". For example, if your name is John Doe, it would say "Hi, John Doe?" with a question mark next to your last name. The fact that Amazon knows your name isn't magic, because if you already have an Amazon Prime account then they will obviously know who it is that purchase the device; however, the question mark is there in the event that this name is not yours. For example, if a loved one bought this device for you as a gift, then you will likely see their name appear on this screen instead of your own. As you can see, you then have the option of determining whether you want to continue as the account that is registered, or if you would prefer to add your own credentials.

You can also see in the picture above the notification saying that if you need to setup your network settings, then you should hit the back button on your

Fire Stick remote. Doing this will take you to a screen where you can activate the Wi-Fi for your device. In order to do this, you must know both the name of your internet network along with the password in order to complete this step. If you have ever setup your internet for a different device in the past, this is going to be basically the same process.

After you've decided which user account you're going to use, you then unfortunately will have to sit through a user video that give you some basic information about the Fire Stick. While this is not stated outright in any direct way, it's relatively safe to say that the primary point of this video is to coerce you into purchasing an Amazon Prime membership if you have not already done so. You cannot skip over this video; if you try to back out of it, it will simply reorient back to where you left off in the video once you try to turn on your device again. Once the video is over, you will be prompted to the home screen, and the setup process is over. You should now be able to the applications that the Fire Stick carries, and we will go into greater detail on how you can choose your preferences in terms of navigating to your favorite applications easily and reliably every time you turn your Fire Stick on.

Hopefully, this chapter has helped you to form a completed picture in your mind about what you have to do in order to take your Amazon Fire Stick from inside of its packaging box and turn it into something that you can use. The two previous chapters in this book were designed to allow you to become generally familiar with the basic installation process of this device. There is still much for you to learn regarding how you can organize your device in an efficient way and other perks that you can utilize once you become familiar with the basics of your device.

Chapter 4: Streaming Shows on Your Device

Now that you know the basics of how to setup your Fire Stick, we're going to start digging deeper into all of the capabilities that this device can offer you and your life. One of the biggest reasons why people decide that they're going to purchase the Fire Stick in the first place is that you're able to stream any TV or movie application on this device. This chapter is going to discuss how you can go about putting yourself in a situation where you are able to watch the best of the best and play the best games that are on the net.

Why You Should Consider an Amazon Prime Membership

Amazon is big on having the other products that they produce work in conjunction with their Prime Membership. Amazon Prime began as a way for members to receive free shipping on all of their orders. Today, Prime has grown to become something that encompasses free shipping along with a plethora of benefits. This includes things like free video streaming, free music streaming, the ability to access a free Amazon Cloud Drive that will store your files, photos and documents for you, and much more. Some other benefits include receiving a thirty-minute window where a particular, hot-selling item will be available to Prime members before they're available to anyone else, access to free Kindle e-books, and also includes Prime Now. Prime Now is a feature where you can purchase goods, food, gifts and groceries and these items will be delivered within two hours for free.

Sorry for barraging you with all of the different benefits of having an Amazon Prime membership, but I know that this book is specifically about the Fire Stick and I want to get back to talking about that. While you should be able to see the many advancements that Amazon is making in many sectors of their industry through what a Prime membership can offer you, once you sign up for Amazon Prime and also own a Fire Stick, you are able to benefit from the free streaming services that they offer. For any of the shows that Amazon itself produces, you are able to view these shows as part of your membership with Amazon Prime. Once you're a Prime member, you also can get rid of any other types of music streaming services to which you may currently be subscribed, such as Spotify or Pandora. The Fire Stick will allow you to stream this music directly from your television, which means that if you ever have a party at your house or even at someone else's house, all you have to do is plug your device into an awaiting television set and let the device do the playlist work for you.

Subscribing to Amazon Prime costs $99 per year. When broken down this comes to roughly $8.50 per year, not including any taxes and other applicable fees. In a simplified world, this means that if you were to purchase an Amazon Fire Stick for $39.99 and then purchase an Amazon Prime membership, you would be paying $138.99 *per year* for television. Take a moment to compare this to the cable subscription for which you're currently paying. This only comes to $11.58 *per year*; however, while Amazon has recently been producing some top-notch shows, it's unlikely that you're going to want to only subscribe to the shows that Amazon Prime offers.

The Concept of an Application

These days, it seems as if every channel that you can find on cable television also has an application that corresponds to the type of shows that are offered on that particular channel. For example, once you install your Fire Stick you will see that the History Channel, Comedy Central, and most of the prominent news networks all have applications that are available for a free download onto your device. What this means for you (and more broadly for the future of the cable television industry) is that you can avoid paying a monthly fee to your cable subscriber and opt instead to download *free* apps that you can find on your Fire Stick. You can still get your daily dose of news and most of the other shows that you watch when you download the channel's app, and if you can't get it for free then you will be able to get it for a small monthly fee.

Sling TV

If having these specific applications still aren't enough to quench your frequent television fix, then you also have the option to subscribe to a service called Sling TV. Sling TV is an application that you will find on your Fire Stick, and it only costs $20 per month. The idea of Sling TV is that it basically allows you to choose the channels that you want on your television without all of the excess channels that you usually get when you purchase cable television. While you get plenty of channel options when you choose the basic cable option, you can also choose an option where you get even more channels for only five dollars more. Hopefully, you can see why this type of technology matters to someone who is sick of paying an expensive cable bill each month. Sling TV allows you to directly engage more with the shows that you're watching and endorsing because you get to pick what goes onto your television. From an entertainment perspective, this forces the cable networks to think about how they can attract your business like never before. Sling TV gives cable networks a way to compete with one another like never before, and as a viewer you're reaping the benefits of this increased competition.

Other Streaming Services

Other streaming services that you may want to consider if you're someone who is looking to stay away from cable television include Netflix, Hulu, HBO, and Showtime. All of these services typically range in price from eight dollars to twenty-five dollars, with Sling TV being one of the more expensive options in which you can invest. While paying for all of these different services may initially seem like a hassle, it's easy to rationale spending this type of money because it is still more than likely going to cost less than the subscribing to a cable service. Additionally, when you spend your money on these types of services, it's likely that you're going to find that the quality of what you're watching has improved immensely. No longer will you be held captive and forced to watch shows that are only subpar. When you pay for a specific streaming service, the quality of show that you're going to receive is going to be far superior to what you're currently watching. This is because these streaming services typically have more revenue available to invest in show production.

As should be obvious after reading this chapter, it's more than likely that you'll have to purchase applications upon purchasing your Amazon Fire Stick if you are not already subscribed to streaming services. If you're someone who is not subscribed to any services currently, the best option for you might be to purchase an Amazon Prime membership. As was previously stated, Prime members can receive many benefits that go beyond streaming services. Additionally, since you've already invested in a Fire Stick, then it would make sense that you also own a Prime Membership. Let's say that you're someone who does not want to pay for more than one streaming services.

With a Prime Membership, you're able to watch not only the television shows that Amazon offers via their own production methods; you'll also be able to stream all of the movies that come with a Prime Membership as well as music options. While it would certainly be nice if I could tell you that once you spend the forty-dollars on the Fire Stick, you would not have to spend any more money, this is simply not the case. If you don't purchase at least one of the applications that were described in this chapter or find a different application that was not discussed, your Fire Stick is going to be likely useless. The best advice to follow when you're seeking to use your Fire Stick if you've never used a device like this before is to start with purchasing one application and go from there. There are no contracts or obligations when you're using any of these applications, so if you don't like it and would like to try a different service, you easily have that option. That's another perk that speaks to the direction in which the entertainment industry is moving. Consumers have more choices, and your choice of applications on your streaming device is concrete evidence of this fact.

Chapter 5: Alexa and the Amazon Fire Stick

Now that you're aware of the streaming capabilities of the Fire Stick and what needs to be done on your part in order for the Fire Stick to stream the shows and movies that you want, we are now going to look at how you can use Amazon's voice-activation technology in conjunction with your device. Most readers have probably heard of Alexa, but in case you haven't, Alexa is a service that was introduced to the world by Amazon around the time of Christmas 2016 (conveniently). While Amazon did come out with a voice-activation remote control for the Fire Stick prior to the development of Alexa, the technology that Alexa represents goes well beyond anything that has been introduced in the past. This chapter will briefly look at the capabilities of Alexa, and more importantly will look into the cost of integrating this type of technology into the Fire Stick that you already own. By the end of this chapter, you'll be able to use all of capabilities that Alexa can offer your home and your life with only the press of a button on your Fire Stick remote control.

Alexa Technology and the Development of the Echo

It's important to understand that Alexa is not simply a voice-activated device. Instead, Amazon describes Alexa as a tool that is always gaining knowledge about her user's identity, preferences, and choices. When you have an Alexa in your household, you're able to ask Alexa general questions that she uses the internet to answer for you. You can also ask her questions about the weather, tell her to play specific music for you, and even set up alarms and reminders for you. One of the more significant features of Alexa, perhaps even the most significant feature, is that you can order supplies for your home by simply telling Alexa what you need. For example, if you saw that you were low on toilet paper or paper towels, you could simply say, "Alexa, order twelve rolls of toilet paper" and Amazon would deliver this product to you within a two-day window. If you have ever seen the Disney movie *Smart House*, then you have an idea of the future implications that technology such as the Echo and Alexa device bring with it. For now, an electronic device is available that will deliver goods to you so that you don't have to go to the store. Tomorrow, who knows what this type of technology will be able to do to enhance your life?

Currently, an Echo device for you home, which is what powers Alexa, will cost you $180. This is before any of the accessories that you can buy with this device, such as supplemental devices that you can put in other areas of your home so that you don't even have to walk into the same room each time you want to order something. When you own a Fire Stick device that has Alexa capabilities, it is going to cost you about $140 less than installing an Echo device into your home. That's right, the Alexa remote only costs $45, which means that if you already own a Fire Stick but you want to purchase the Alexa-enabled remote, it is likely only going to cost you between five to ten dollars more than a regular Fire Stick would.

Using Alexa with Your Fire Stick

It's important to recognize that while this book is going to focus on how you can use a Fire Stick and not a Fire TV, the setup for both the Fire Stick and the Fire TV to enable Alexa integration are largely the same. Additionally, it's also important to understand that if you bought a Fire Stick with an Alexa-enabled remote control as part of the package, you still have to know what to do in order to get Alexa to respond on your remote.

As you can see from the picture above, the easiest way to be able to tell whether or not you already own a Fire Stick with Alexa capabilities is to look for the small microphone button on your Fire Stick remote control. If you look and see that this button is on your remote, then Alexa is already enabled on your device; however, because of the fact that you actually need to press this button in order to use Alexa on your Fire Stick, you may or may not have already operated your remote using this feature. Of course, if you don't have a remote that looks like this, consider heading to a technology store and picking up one for roughly $40.

Once you know that you have the proper remote, the next step is to head to your Home screen (remember, all you have to do is press the button on your remote that resembles a house). Once you're at the home screen, press and *hold* the microphone key. It's not enough to simply press the microphone key and let it go. If you do this, then there is no way that the microphone on the remote control will be able to know what you're saying to it. When you hold the microphone button down, you're going to see a "listening..." screen pop up, and this is how you'll know that you can speak into the remote. The listening screen is going to look like the picture that's depicted below.

Say the title, actor, director, or category into the remote's built-in mic to see results

Once you see this screen, you have the option of basically asking Alexa anything that you want. This can relate to television commands such as, "Turn on the Eagles football game", but it can also relate to anything that can be found on the internet as well. You can ask Alexa a question or tell her to turn on the news. The choice is yours. Additionally, when you're finished with one command and want to tell Alexa to do something new, this is where the trusty back button on your remote control will come in handy. If you already own an Echo device and talk to Alexis on the regular, the only difference between talking to Alexa on the Echo and talking to Alexa from your remote control is that you don't have to say "Alexa…" when making a voice command. Instead, when you press the voice command microphone button on your remote control, this is essentially replacing the need to say the device's name. If you already own the remote control and would like to try out some more of the features that it can offer you, it might be a good idea to head over to the Settings section of your device. From here, go to Applications, and then Alexa, and then the Things to Try tab. This will show you some of the other features that can be activated with your voice. These features include gaining access to audiobooks, calendars, facts, and much more.

It's important to understand that if you own a remote control that has the option to be manipulated by voice but do not have an Amazon Prime account, then you are going to be able to use Alexa in the way that was just described above. Essentially, when you use Alexa in any way, this is directly connected to an account that Amazon provides for you through a Prime membership. While it would be nice to think that you could magically order goods online like paper towel rolls and detergent without having to pay for them, this is simply not the case. The remote control option for the Fire Stick is yet another reason why you should be considering purchasing an Amazon Prime Membership. The breakthrough of this innovative technology makes it easy to see how Amazon is paving the way of the future, and Alexa's ability to integrate with the Amazon Fire Stick is yet even more proof of this fact.

Chapter 6: Tips on How to Get the Most from Your Fire Stick Device

Up until this point in the book, we have discussed large topics regarding the Fire Stick device that you may find useful. This chapter is different in the sense that instead of talking about one over-arching topic, we are instead going to be discussing a variety of topics that will take your ability to use your Fire Stick to the next level. These topics include enabling yourself to watch your Fire Stick in different rooms of the house without having to purchase additional televisions, and how to connect your smartphone to your Fire Stick so that you can talk to it without the voice remote if this is something that you don't want to purchase. Even from just reading this opening paragraph, it should be obvious that the options that you have are almost endless in terms of how you can customize your device in a way that will meet your needs exactly.

Use Miracast to Make Any Portable Device Fire Stick-Friendly

Miracast is an application that will allow essentially allow you to mirror your television's image directly to a smartphone or tablet without the use of any physical HDMI cables. In order for screen mirroring to work on your device, one of the first things that you need to know is that you will not be able to use Miracast with an iPhone. Only Windows products or Android products will work in conjunction with this application and a Fire Stick. After you've made sure that the particular device that you want to pair with the Miracast is compatible, click and hold the Home button on your Fire Stick remote control. When you hold this button down, it will bring you to a screen where you will be able to click on an option that's labeled "Mirroring". From here, you will be able to select your portable device from the list of options that are available on your television. When you're finished mirroring the television show to your portable device, you can click any button on your Fire Stick remote control and this will end the mirroring session.

While the instructions that were provided above may sound relatively simple, there are a few additional details that you should be keeping in mind as you seek to sync your Fire Stick device with Miracast. For example, a common mistake that people make when they're pairing to Miracast is that they forget to put their portable device on the same Wi-Fi that is connected to their Fire Stick. If the Fire Stick and the portable device are not on the same Wi-Fi connection, then they basically will not be able to communicate with one another. Additionally, you need to make sure that when you're first pairing Miracast with your portable device the television that's connected to your Fire Stick that you're within at least thirty feet of your television. While you should be able to move to a different area of your home after your device is connected to Miracast, you will have to make sure that you're within the specified thirty-feet distance of the television that's connected to the Fire Stick while you're setting it up.

Making Your Fire Stick Compatible with Apple Products

If you're someone who is more allegiant to Apple products than you are Android products, not all hope is lost. One of the great aspects of the Fire Stick is that you can customize in almost any way that you see fit. When you're looking to make your Fire Stick compatible with Apple products, you will first need to download an application that's called AirPlay/DLNA Receiver (PRO). It's important to note here that there are other applications on the market that claim to offer mirroring compatibility with Apple products; however, many of them are not exactly full-proof or truthful in their capabilities. The AirPlay/DLNA Receiver (PRO) is going to cost you $4.99 upon download, but for many people this is a small price to pay in order to be able to watch television in bed or in the kitchen while cooking meals without having to pay the $150 that Apple charges for their Apple TV product. It's safe to say that a five-dollar one-time fee will beat a one-time $150 fee any day of the week.

Pairing Your Smartphone to Fire Stick Remote Control

If you're someone who purchased a Fire Stick before the development of the voice-activated remote option was introduced to the public, then you may be (understandably) a bit hesitant to run out and spend an extra forty-dollars on an Alexa-enabled remote. When you think about it, your smartphone works similarly to the remote control that Amazon now sells. It has voice activation capabilities, and its touch-screen technology can essentially work the same way that a remote does. Of course, the developers of the Amazon Fire Stick recognized this, and they did what any reputable technology would do when there was a customer need that is to be filled in some way. They developed an application for it.

If you want to save some money and download a voice-activated Fire Stick rather than purchase one, the application that you're going to want to download is called the "Amazon Fire TV Remote" application (pretty creative name, right?). You can download this at any app store that's on your smartphone. Additionally, prior to downloading this application, you're going to want to make sure that you're using either a portable device that is an Amazon or an Android product and is a version 4.0 or higher, or that you're using an Apple product that is at least a version 7 or higher. This certainly limits the types of devices that are able to turn into a remote control. Obviously, you will have no choice but to purchase a new remote control from Amazon if your smartphone is older than the ones described above.

When you're installing this application on your phone, you're going to want to make sure that your smartphone is connected to the same Wi-Fi to which your television is connected. Once the application is finished installing on your phone, it will prompt you to find the Fire Stick device with which you're looking to pair. Once the two devices are paired with one another, you can then navigate this remote in the same manner that you would navigate your traditional Amazon remote.

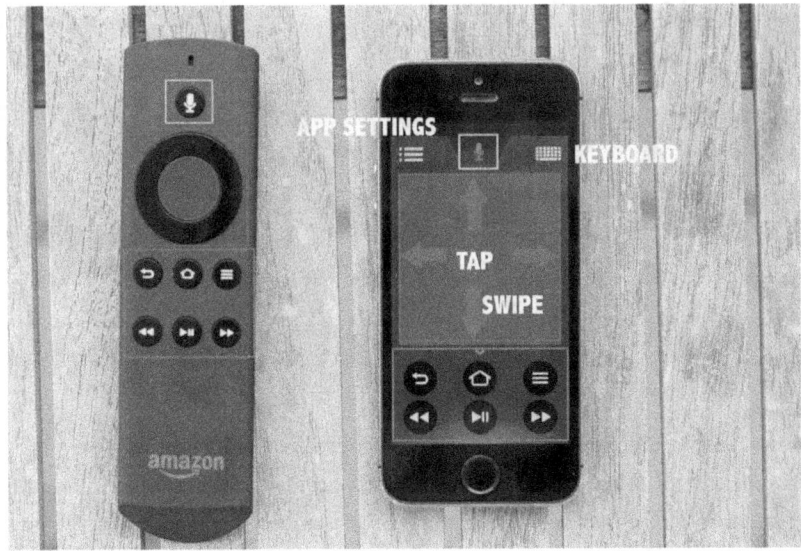

While we're not going to go through all of the button options that you have for your remote again, the picture above is helpful because it provides you with an idea of what the remote is going to look like once you've downloaded it to your phone. As you can see, in the top middle of the phone that's in the photo, there is a microphone and this works the same as the button on the Amazon remote. Simply press and hold this button and then talk into the spot on your phone where the speaker is located.

While everything else on the mobile remote control is basically the same as the physical remote control that you can buy from Amazon, we need to discuss the swiping that needs to be done on your portable device. Instead of the physical navigation button that is the dark black circle on the Amazon remote control, you will have top swipe on your phone in order to navigate left, right, up and down. The various pictures below should help to clarify this point.

Two last important points about the smartphone configuration for the remote control on the Fire Stick involve the keyboard capabilities and removing your mobile device as a remote on your Fire Stick once it's been installed. When you install the remote control on your smartphone, you're able to also use your keyboard to type in the actions that you want to perform or get to the place that you want to get to on your television. If you're someone who is not exactly computer savvy and like to type in your results rather than swipe or press buttons to get to them, then this may be a reason why you would consider downloading the application onto your phone rather than purchasing the product.

On the other hand, it's also important to note that once you download the remote control application onto your smartphone, there is no way that you can remove it from being paired with your television. The only way to remove your smartphone is to reset your Fire Stick back to its factory settings. If you're rather tech savvy and know a thing or two about how to use applications, then you might be someone who has already customized your Fire Stick to the fullest extent possible. If this is the case, then it's safe to say that it would be a hassle for you to reset your device to its factory settings because doing so would require you to put in a lot of work to get your Fire Stick back to its customized settings. These two details are important to think about before deciding whether you're going to purchase the remote from Amazon or download it onto your phone.

Chapter 7: The Controversial Kodi Application and How to Use It

Hopefully, the previous chapter was able to provide you with some information on how you can optimize the use of your Amazon Fire Stick without having to spend any additional money on streaming applications or hardware such as televisions or tablets. This next chapter is going to go beyond even some of the technical topics that we discussed in the previous chapter. Instead, we are going to move towards the most advanced topic that you'll find in this book, which is the Kodi application. We'll discuss what the Kodi is, what it does, why it's controversial, and how you can easily install it on your Fire Stick. If you're someone who does not worry much about the ethics that surround entertainment copywriting, then there is no reason why you shouldn't be using the Kodi.

The Notion of Open-Source Software

At it's core, Kodi can be best defined as a type of software that is open-source in nature. What this means is that the rights to the Kodi software have been publicly distributed by whoever created the product in the first place, and this material can be distributed and manipulated by the public. From this perspective, open-source software is largely to be considered collaborative, because once the programming code of the software is given to other programmers, these people then manipulate the code collectively and enhance its operation. No one "owns" this software, yet it's generally agreed that people will work together to improve the development of this software.

Now that you have idea of what the concept of open-source software means, we can get into the details of the open-source nature of Kodi influences its userability. Kodi was originally designed to be used on the Xbox, but its community of developers soon expanded and the Kodi application itself grew with it. Today, Kodi is operated by over 500 developers all over the world who speak a variety of languages have a wide range of programming skills. This type of diversity that exists within the ranks of the Kodi has allowed it to expand into something greater than it was when it was first developed back in 2003.

What Does Kodi Do?

When it was first built, Kodi was designed to turn any computer into a device that could stream *any* content onto a television with ease. Today, it's also possible for the Kodi to achieve this same goal on smartphones and tablets, although it's important to note that the kinks for this type of Kodi use are still being worked out. Because the Fire Stick has larger memory storage than some types of tablets and smartphones, it has become a prime target for the Kodi market. Essentially, any Android device is Kodi-compatible, but Apple porducts are not because they need to be jailbroken before they're able to use Kodi.

Kodi is useful on devices like the Fire Stick because it enables you to gain access to copywritten material for which you'd otherwise have to pay. Most notably, this includes sporting events that you would have to pay a subcription fee to view and also includes movies that have been uploaded to the internet for free-viewing. While we will discuss how to install Kodi in the next section of this chapter, it's important to understand that once the installation process is complete, you're going to still need to download applications onto your Kodi product in order to gain access to the free streaming services that are available. Kodi calls their applications, "add-ons" instead of apps, and these can be easily downloaded once you have installed Kodi to your Amazon Fire Stick. Let's take a look at some of the best add-ons that Kodi offers its users.

1. **Specto:** If you've ever used torrents and have downloaded files from torrent sites like the pirate bay, then you know that these websites can sometimes be a bit...racey. The same can be said for Kodi if you're not careful while browsing. When you install the add-on called Specto onto your Kodi device, you are making it possible for your kids to stream cartoon shows and other programs that are suitable for viewers of all ages. If you have kids or know that your Fire Stick will be

catering to a younger audience, Specto is definately something you should consider using.

2. **Exodus:** The creators of the Exodus application had previously produced an application called Genesis, but unfortunately this application became unusable. People who had taken the time to download Genesis ended up being sent to dead links and other entrapments within the Genesis network, and this led to the creation of Exodus. Today, Exodus is arguably the most popular Kodi application on the market, because of the fact that it's able to piece multiple streams of audio and digital files together and create a cohesive film or television show to watch. Additionally, almost all of the media that you can watch on Exodus also gives you the option to view it in HD, which also contributes to its popularity.

3. **1Channel Primewire:** 1Channel Primewire, while it requires some customization, is largely considered to be one of the only other add-ons that you need to download to your Kodi in conjunction with either Exodus of Specto. While Exodus and Specto can provide you with all of the movies and televison shows you could ever watch for free on the internet, 1Channel Primewire can provide you with the games and other applications that the internet can provide you.

Installing Kodi on Your Fire Stick Device

If you're looking for a way to reap almost all of the rewards that the internet can offer, then you should be looking to install Kodi on your Fire Stick. The first thing that you want to do when you're looking to install Kodi is to browse to the follow location, starting at the home page for your Fire Stick:

1. Settings
2. Developer Options
3. Apps from Unknown Sources – turn this option "on"

While you're browsing to the "Apps from Unknown Sources" section of the Fire Stick, you also have the option of turning on your ADB Debugging feature so that you can access additional applications more easily in the future. Once you have the correct settings activated, you can hit the home button on your remote so that you're back on the home screen. Next, move towards the search bar that's on the home page and type in, "Downloader". The Kodi downloader will then pop-up on your screen, and once you hit download the application will start writing to your Fire Stick. After the downloader has been going for a bit, a box will appear that will prompt you to do the follow: "Enter the URL of the file you want to download." This URL is the following:

http://troypoint.com/kodistable

Click next after you're finished typing in this URL. Again, you will click the download button so that the Fire Stick knows that it is going to download this particular URL. Once it's finished downloading, it's important to launch Kodi and make sure that it's working properly. After the installation process is complete, you can look to add-on some or all of the popular applications that have already been discussed in this chapter.

While installing Kodi on your Fire Stick device is not exactly "traditional" in the sense that you're going to be navigating a space that is "off the grid" in terms of how the typical user uses their Fire Stick, this should not necessarily deter you from attempting to install Kodi onto your device. Another way to look at this is to think about how cheap the Fire Stick costs. Compared to many other streaming devices, the Fire Stick ranks among the cheaper streaming options. If you're nervous about how well you're going to install an application such as Kodi, if you make a mistake and somehow make the device unusable, it's unlikely that you won't be able to afford another Fire Stick in the near future.

Lastly, it's important to discuss the controversy surrounding Kodi so that you have a clear understanding of how Kodi tip-toes around copyright infringement. Kodi essentially allows you to stream videos, television shows, sports networks and other types of copywritten material without the consent of the people who originally captured and own the content. For example, one of the most profitable ways for sport networks to make money on the games that are played by various sports teams is to charge membership fees for these game channels. For people who are getting rid of their cable, the inability to easily watch sports is one of the reasons why they will choose to pay for subscriptions to Sling TV or the ESPN Network. Kodi completely eliminates the need to subscribe to basically any streaming service that offers unique forms of visual entertainment. It can be hard to stop these types of free streaming services because of the fact that open-source software is often decentralized. If the fact that there are some lawsuits against the use of Kodi doesn't bother you or you're someone who has ripped information from the internet before in a similar manner, then it's safe to say that Kodi is a must-have for anyone who is serious about getting the most free content from their Fire Stick. While it may be a bit of a complicated process, using Kodi is definately worth the time it takes to install it, as long as you're relatively good with computer technology and know that you won't be too upset if something ends up going wrong.

Conclusion

Thank for making it through to the end of *Fire Stick: Easy to Advanced Tips and Tricks to Get the MOST Out of Your Device, an In-Depth PICTURE Guide for ALL! (Streaming Devices, Amazon Fire Stick User Guide, how to Use Fire Stick)*, let's hope it was informative and able to provide you with all of the tools you need to achieve your goals whatever it may be.

The next step is to either continue to research the Amazon Fire Stick in relation to other streaming devices that are on the market, or if you're confident in the ability of the Fire Stick after reading this book then you should go out and purchase the Fire Stick as soon as you can! Hopefully, this book has shown you the countless capabilities that the Fire Stick can offer to enhance your life, and there's no reason why you shouldn't allow this device to provide you with a cheaper mode of entertainment.

www.ingramcontent.com/pod-product-compliance
Lightning Source LLC
Chambersburg PA
CBHW071309280526
45788CB00004B/1863